TABLE OF CONTENTS

A	Adjusting Anna Changing Family	6
B	Belonging Ben Teamwork and Community	10
C	Changing Charlie Creating Healthy Habits	14
D	Direct Dalia Gossip	18
E	Encouraging Eddie Leadership	22
F	Faking It Fran Self-Confidence	26
G	Grateful Gretta Gratitude	30
H	Home Organizer Hal Organization	34
I	Inspiring Izzie Finding Your Passion	38
J	PreJUDGED Jamal Diversity	42
K	Kind Karen Kindness	46
L	Listening Lucy Listening	50
M	Mannerly Mike Manners	54
N	Noticing Naima Anxiety	58
O	Optimistic Oreda Positive Thinking	62
P	Pausing Pablo Coping with Anger	66
Q	Quieting Quin Calming Skills	70
R	Reporting Roxy Tattling vs. Reporting	74
S	Stand Up Stella Standing up for Others & Yourself	78
T	Tenacious Tim Problem Solving	82
U	Unmovable Uriel Peer Pressure	86
V	Valuing Van Goal Setting	90
W	Wondrous Will Grieving	94
X	Extra Effort Xaiden Study Skills	98
Y	Yessing Yula Taking Risks	102
Z	Zoned In Zeb Focusing	106

Breathe and Stretch

Focus on the now.
Breathe through nose filling up lungs fully
with oxygen and exhale through nose slowly.
Feel your chest expand.
Keep your eyes on one object and ignore distractions.
Smile & never give up!
Feel calm inside.

1. MOUNTAIN POSE: Stand tall with hands reaching to the sky. Breathe here for 5-10 breaths.

2. SINGLE KNEE RAISE: Lift right knee while keeping both hands raised above you. Stay here for 5-10 breaths.

3. AIRPLANE POSE: Slowly, sail your right leg back for airplane. Hands come to side. Stay here for 5-10 breaths. Keep your heart lifted.

4. EAGLE POSE. Bring right leg back to front and wrap it around your left leg. Stay standing on your left leg firmly. Bring your right arm under your left arm and grasp hands. Lift your elbows up to chin level and sit your hips down 6 inches. Stay here for 5-10 breaths.

5. SWITCH TO OTHER SIDE. Repeat 1-4 on the other side of your body.

6. WIDE LEGGED FORWARD BEND: Widen legs and slowly bend body over. Allow head to hang like a coconut on a tree. Reach right arm to left ankle and stretch left arm to sky. Twist here for 5-10 breaths and switch sides.

Slowly roll your spine up to mountain pose and breathe.

Visit powerfulyou.info for more breathing and stretching activities.

The Story of Powerful You
By Mrs. Frizzi

Powerful You began many years ago when I discovered the power of storytelling as a guidance counselor. Children begged for me to lay aside my guidance lesson plans and retell the true stories of my former students. After introducing Stand-Up Stella, children began walking taller and standing up for themselves. I saw how children who were experiencing changes at home were comforted meeting Adjusting Anna as they began opening up and sharing hidden emotions. Others practiced tips on the playground that Tenacious Tim taught.

As I learned from the children by listening to them during reflection time, I realized that all children cope with challenges in different ways. I wanted to provide more children with the tools to develop a Powerful You. After completing a yoga teacher training, I knew it was time to document and share the power that each incredible child held inside.

The following A-Z true stories have been collected during my 30+ years of working as an educator in actual classrooms. These stories and activities will empower children to create the life they want, regardless of what has happened to them. Everything they need to shine is already inside.

About Mrs. Frizzi

Mrs. Frizzi was born on a small Indiana farm. She learned at a young age to create the life she wanted. Her parents and seven siblings lived in a two-bedroom home surrounded by a beautiful forest. She discovered early her love for nature and simple living. Although she was told she could never go to college, she secretly applied and continued writing her life. After proudly graduating from Ball State University with an education degree, she moved to Southwest Florida. The need to help underprivileged children inspired her to get a masters degree in counseling from the University of South Florida. She continued working with her husband for over 30 years, educating and counseling children. When her own children left for college, she also became a yoga instructor and currently enjoys inspiring others to love yoga.

You can find Mrs. Frizzi sailing with her hubby on the Gulf of Mexico, practicing yoga on her paddleboard, or trying to open a coconut for her smoothie. She loves special moments with her two Florida-grown children. Go Gators and Noles!

Adjusting Anna

A ADJUSTING Anna

"Have you ever had a huge change in your life where you felt everything was falling apart? In fourth grade my life turned upside down. My parents used to live together but then moved to different houses, and my dad moved to a new state. At first I was so angry. 'How could my parents do this to me? Who will I live with? Will I still get to see my friends? Will I get to see my dad?' My anger changed to sadness over time. I couldn't concentrate on my schoolwork. Finally, I visited with my school counselor, and she taught me the 3 C's of change. I didn't CAUSE it, I surely can't CONTROL it, but I can learn to COPE with the change. I started eating lunch and playing with a group of kids who were going through similar changes. After many weeks of feeling lonely, I slowly began to adjust and find my smile again. Now I can spot others going through difficulties and know just how to help them find their shine again."

POSITIVE SELF-TALK
"I adjust to change."

REFLECT & SHINE

- Every new school year you adjust to a different teacher, friends, and schoolwork. Name a school change that has been difficult.

- Have you had any changes at home that have been difficult? How did you feel?

- What friend or family member in your life has listened to you during these times? What did they say or do that comforted you?

- What is something you wished your teacher knew about you?

~ ACTIVITIES ~

"When you can't adjust the direction of the wind, adjust your sails."
– H. Jackson Brown, Jr.

3 C'S OF CHANGE:
» I didn't CAUSE it.   » I can't CONTROL it.   » But I can learn to COPE.

Control: Fill in the box with things you can and can't control.

	Control	Can't Control		Control	Can't Control
stormy weather	☐	☐	your actions	☐	☐
your attitude	☐	☐	teachers	☐	☐
clothes you wear	☐	☐	your smile	☐	☐
grumpy friends	☐	☐	how you look at things	☐	☐
the past	☐	☐	your words	☐	☐
the future	☐	☐	your body	☐	☐
your thoughts	☐	☐	parents moving	☐	☐
fighting parents	☐	☐	unhealthy habits	☐	☐

The Oreo Cookie Club: If you have a friend who is going through changes at home, give them an Oreo cookie. Twist it open gently. One side is the mom, and one side is the dad. Both sides are apart, but the good stuff is the white, fluffy yummy cream in the middle. That is YOU!! All parents would agree that YOU are the good stuff that happened in the family. Enjoy your cookie!

Color Clouds
When changes happen in a home, you might feel these colorful emotions:

- Blue (sad)
- Red (anger)
- Yellow (happy)
- Green (jealous)
- Orange (worry)
- Mixed colors (confused)

Draw clouds and color according to how you feel. Draw x-large clouds for stronger feelings and small clouds for small feelings.

Belonging
Ben

B BELONGING — Ben

"I love every minute I am on the soccer field. When I was young my coach would yell, 'Ben, pass the ball to your teammates!' Scoring a goal was my passion, and I was determined to win the game for my team. As I grew older, I realized that it took every player on the field to score a goal, not just me. I needed my teammate's support. This idea has carried over to every part of my life. In school, every student is needed during discussions. In Boy Scouts, everyone brings strength and weakness to campouts. At home, we must work together to keep our house clean. Working together and supporting each other is fun and creates community."

POSITIVE SELF-TALK
"I belong and contribute."

REFLECT & SHINE

- Being connected to a group of people helps you feel safe. Name different groups that people belong to:

- Your family is a community that supports you. What does your family do that makes you feel safe and loved? How do they support you?

- How can you help people on your team or class feel important? How do you support your family?

- If you could join any group, which one would you join?

~ ACTIVITIES ~

"TEAM = Together Everyone Achieves More!"

"The greatest thing about teamwork is that you always have others on your side."
— Margaret Carty

TEAM-BUILDING HULA-HOOP:

» Gather friends, stand in a circle, and hold hands. Place one hula-hoop over one pair of joined hands. Each person in the circle must pass the hoop over him/herself and on to the next person while staying connected at all times.

Supported Tree Pose: Create a large circle.

Stand tall on left foot. Bend your right knee and bring your right foot on the inside of your left leg. Bring your right foot up as high as possible. Press your right knee out towards person next to you on right. Lift arms overhead to form a "V". Hold hands with person next to you for support. Stay here and breathe for 5-10 audible, focused breaths. Be still and listen to the breaths while supporting each other. Switch to the opposite side.

Family Fun:

It can be difficult for families to make a meal and clean up.

Turn this big task into fun. All members choose the meal to cook.

Everyone has a part in:

- Scrubbing
- Cutting
- Mixing
- Washing
- Pouring
- Setting
- Cleaning
- Turn on some music, find a song you all love, and have fun.

Changing Charlie

CHANGING Charlie

"Do you love to sit in front of your video games, eat potato chips, and drink soda? It's what made me happy until the day I ran a race on field day. I was the last one to cross the finish line. I felt humiliated! I looked in the mirror and asked myself, 'Why do you feel so horrible?' That is when I decided to take charge of my life. I began drinking crystal clear water and eating colorful fruits and vegetables. I discovered I felt better when I played basketball instead of sitting in my room playing video games. Breathing in fresh air gave me energy that I loved. Changing a few unhealthy habits helped me shine bright."

 { **POSITIVE SELF-TALK** "I create healthy habits." }

REFLECT & SHINE

- Your body needs eight glasses of water a day in order to hydrate your cells. What can you do to increase your water intake?

- Never touch your eyes or mouth with your unwashed hands. Why?

- Why is it healthy to keep your fingernails clipped short?

- Your amazing body needs 8-10 hours of sleep each night. How many hours of sleep do you get? What helps you fall asleep at night?

- What fun outdoor activity do you enjoy?

~ ACTIVITIES ~

"Creating Change"

"You are 100% responsible for who you are regardless of what has happened to you."
– Jack Canfield

HEALTHY HABITS:
» Drinking 8 glasses of water daily
» Eating 4-5 fruits & vegetables daily
» Eating a high protein breakfast
» Playing sports
» Sneezing into your sleeve
» Dancing
» Reading
» Biking
» Running
» Washing hands before eating
» Throwing used tissues in trash
» Walking & talking
» When sad, telling yourself, " I AM AWESOME"
» Getting 8-10 hours of sleep

UNHEALTHY HABITS:
» Drinking soda instead of water
» TOO much TV
» TOO many video games
» Eating candy & potato chips before meals
» Snacking when sad
» Nail biting
» Sharing hats/cups with others
» Putting yourself down
» Staying up late on school nights

CREATING CHANGE CHART

I will keep_____

I will start_____

I will stop_____

Powerful You Bracelet:
Every time you notice yourself doing a healthy habit, change your bracelet to the other wrist. While you are changing the bracelet, take deep breaths and say to yourself, "I am powerful and in control."

Reward Yourself:
When you are able to follow your CREATING CHANGE CHART, make sure you CELEBRATE! What is something you would like to give yourself for being in control?

_____
_____

Direct Dalia

D DIRECT — Dalia

"My good friend, Sue, was mad at me for not replying to a text message she sent. She was hurt at the thought I was ignoring her. Instead of speaking directly to me, she went to all my friends and talked to them about me. Some kids started saying I was unfriendly and stuck up. I went directly to Sue and talked to her. She did not know my parents took my phone away. I wish she'd spoken directly to me when the problem happened instead of gossiping and creating drama. Talking directly to people is sometimes scary, but it quickly solves problems with honesty and communication.
Being honest and direct, in a kind way, allows you to shine!"

POSITIVE SELF-TALK
"I am direct and honest with my words."

REFLECT & SHINE

- Drama happens when friends pass on untrue or negative words about others. Why do people join in on gossip and drama?

- What damage can be done by gossip?

- What can you do to avoid getting involved in gossip?

- Honesty is always the best policy. Lies cause everyone to suffer. Tell about a time you were not 100% honest.

- Whispering hurts. Why is it unkind to whisper with friends when you are with a group?

~ ACTIVITIES ~

"Whoever gossips to you, will gossip about you."
— Spanish Proverb

A lot of problems in the world would be solved if we would talk TO each other instead of ABOUT each other.

WHAT SHOULD YOU DO?

Sandy is telling other girls that Gretta is mean. You are friends with both girls. What should you do?

a. Go to Gretta and tell her that Sandy is talking bad about her.
b. Go to Sandy and tell her to talk directly to Gretta instead of talking bad about her.
c. Join Sandy and learn all about Gretta's problems.

Sandy is mad at you because you did not invite her to your sleepover. What should you do?

a. Hide from Sandy when you see her so you don't have to talk. (going around the problem)
b. Go directly to Sandy and honestly explain that your mom only allows you to have one friend over, and you want her to come another time.
c. Lie and say that you didn't have any friends over.

Telephone:

Form a large circle. Start with gossip and "pass it on" by whispering the gossip to someone next to you. Watch the gossip grow and become drama.

Example: "Did you hear Eddie didn't do his homework last night and got in big, bad trouble with his parents?"

3 Ways to Respond to Others:

1. AGGRESSIVELY or like a monster - "YOU MAKE ME MAD," as you pound your fist!

2. PASSIVELY or like a mouse - "I don't care," as you cry under your breath.

3. DIRECTLY - Say what you want in a polite manner.

Encouraging Eddie

E ENCOURAGING Eddie

"When I moved to my new school I wanted everyone to like me. I thought if I was silly during class, kids would think I was funny and want to play with me. My silliness resulted in a trip to the principal's office. Instead of the kids liking me, they started avoiding me. One even told me I was annoying. Fortunately, kickball saved me. I used my skills to encourage others who were struggling at recess. I built up others who wanted to quit the game by shouting, 'DON'T GIVE UP - KEEP TRYING!' I believe you can do whatever you put your mind to doing. Suddenly kids were asking me to play with them at recess. Becoming a leader by encouraging others helped me SHINE in my new class."

 **POSITIVE SELF-TALK**
"I encourage others to not give up."

REFLECT & SHINE

- Many kids try to fit in by goofing off and acting silly in class. What other ways can you "fit in"?

- "Good Job" is an encouraging statement. What other encouraging statements can you use with friends?

- Who encourages you?

- Annoying habits can cause kids to avoid you. What annoying habits do you notice in yourself?

~ ACTIVITIES ~

"I encourage others."

"Leaders become great, not because of their power, but because of their ability to empower others."
– John Maxwell

"Be kind, for everyone you meet is fighting a hard battle."
– John Watson

ARE YOU AN ENCOURAGING FRIEND?
Put an E in front of encouraging actions

- _____ Shouts, "YOU CAN DO IT!"
- _____ Helps others when they are frustrated.
- _____ Refuses to share.
- _____ Shows off for getting best grade in class.
- _____ Notices effort in others.
- _____ Accepts others for who they are.
- _____ Allows others to have friends.
- _____ Finds the good in others.
- _____ Interested in others' feelings.
- _____ Celebrates accomplishments of others.
- _____ Disrupts the class.
- _____ Shouts, "NEVER GIVE UP!"
- _____ Tells winning team, "GOOD GAME."
- _____ Helps others to believe in themselves.
- _____ Brings positive energy to others.
- _____ Brags to losing team, "WE ARE BETTER THAN YOU."
- _____ Views unwanted CHANGE as an opportunity.
- _____ Blames others with a pointed finger.
- _____ Acknowledges and appreciates others.
- _____ Finds fault in others.

Fran
Faking It

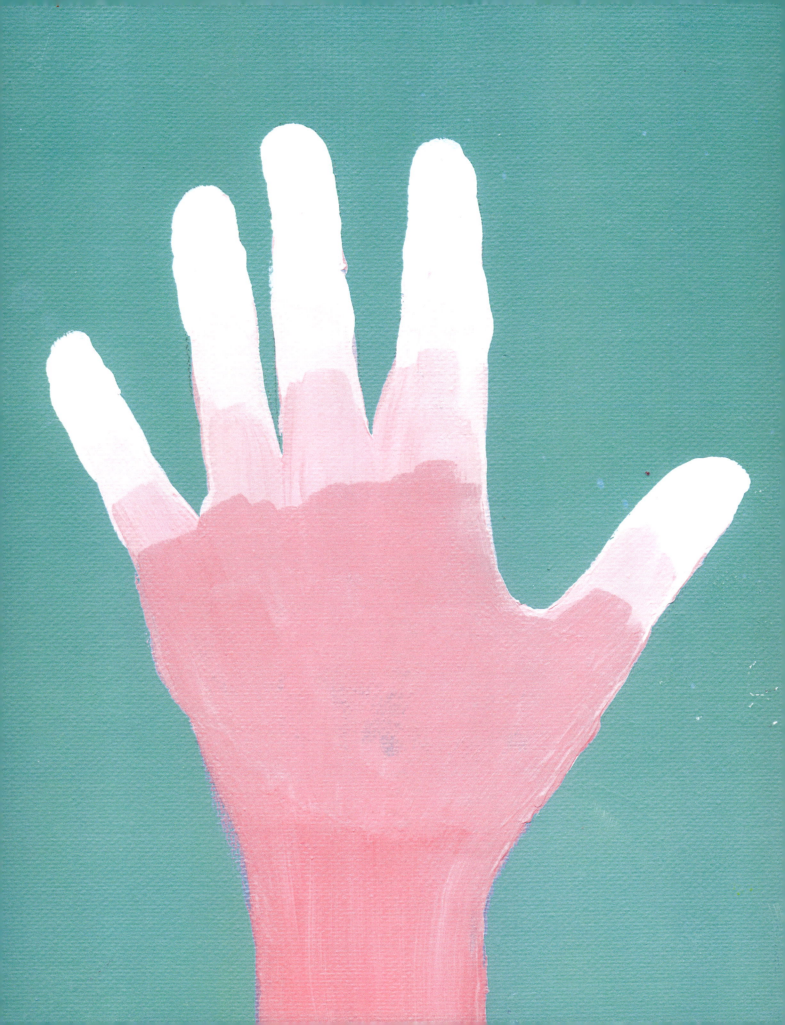

F FAKING IT — Fran

"I refused to raise my hand in class because I was afraid people would laugh at my answer. When I looked in the mirror, I saw a girl who looked like she was scared of her shadow. My body language shouted to the world, 'Pick on me and I will cry.' My parents called my teacher for help. My teacher taught me to 'fake it until I become it.' I practiced standing tall and walking with a smile on my face. Speaking clearly instead of mumbling was difficult at first, but it has become easier with practice. Every morning I look in the mirror and say, 'I AM FRAN AND I AM A BIG DEAL.' Slowly, I have become a confident student who walks tall, speaks firm, and smiles at the world. It usually smiles back!"

POSITIVE SELF-TALK
"I fake it until I become it."

REFLECT & SHINE

- Why must you like yourself in order to be a good friend to others?

- If you had a magic wand, what would you change about yourself? Can you change it? (If not, learn to love it with all your heart.)

- What is something that has been difficult for you?

- What special talents do you share with the world?

~ ACTIVITIES ~

"No one can make you feel inferior
without your consent."
– Eleanor Roosevelt

"It's not your job to like me... it is mine." - Byron Katie

YOU ARE SPECIAL PLATE:

>> Write in permanent black marker around the outer rim of a red paper plate "YOU ARE SPECIAL." Enjoy lunch on your plate and celebrate your uniqueness. Who can you appreciate by serving their lunch on a "YOU ARE SPECIAL" red plate?

Powerful You: Trace your hand on a piece of paper. Write your name in the center of the hand and decorate. On each finger write:

1) One thing you do for fun.
2) Something nice your friends or family would say about you.
3) One thing you like about yourself.
4) One job you could see yourself doing in the future.
5) Something others don't know about you.

Are you Fake or UNIQUE?

F- Focuses on looking good on the outside instead of looking good on the inside.
A- Always wants to impress others and needs lots of PEOPLE APPROVAL.
K- Kindness only goes to people who will give something back.
E- Enjoys pretending to be like someone else.

U- Unplugs for fun outdoor activities.
N- Notices others who are different and compliments them.
I- Invites new people into the group.
Q- Questions why others won't try something new.
U- Understands that looking people in the eye and smiling are valuable.
E- Entertains viewpoints of others.

Grateful Gretta

G GRATEFUL → Gretta

"When I was five years old, my dad was taken away in a police car. I was forced to live in a foster home until my mom was allowed to take care of my sister and me. During those eight, long months while my mom was learning to be a better parent, I did not sleep. I dreamed of her coming through the door with my dog. My foster family took amazing care of me and helped me through a hard time, but I always missed my mom. The day I returned to my mom, I promised myself to always be grateful. Instead of grumbling about what I did not have, I found joy in nature. I love to listen to the birds in the morning with my dog and watch the colorful sunsets at night. Writing thank you notes to those who have helped me in life is important to me. Difficult times have taught me to appreciate small moments in life and know that each day is a gift."

POSITIVE SELF-TALK
"I know each day is a gift."

REFLECT & SHINE

- People say money can't buy happiness. Name five FREE things that bring happiness in your life.

- Spending time with people you love is the best gift you can give others. Who do you need to thank? How do you spend time with them?

- There are things in life that bring you joy. What would you buy that brings joy?

- What do you do to enjoy nature?

~ ACTIVITIES ~

"Each day is a gift."

"Yesterday is history. Tomorrow is a mystery. Today is a gift. That's why we call it "the Present." - Eleanor Roosevelt

GRATEFUL TREE:

» Place a tree branch from your yard in a vase or jar. Cut small leaves out of paper. On each leaf write one thing for which you are thankful. Put a heart next to those words that do not cost money. Hang leaves on a piece of yarn from the tree branch. Involve friends and family for laughter and fun.

Grateful Notes:

Write a thank you note to someone who has been nice to you. It can be as simple as:

Dear_____, Thank you for _____. It made my day.
Love, _____.

Gratitude Bags:

Place the following objects in a small jewelry bag and explain their special meaning to someone you care about.

Pencil: "You are the author of your life."
Smartie: "Everyone has different smarts."
Eraser: "Mistakes are for learning."
Cut out Heart: "Give kindness to everyone you meet."
Birthday cake candle: "Let your light shine."
Other items: Picture of yourself, stickers, favorite poem, special note...

Wash the car for your family: Do you know the fun you could have taking care of this special car that takes you so many cool places? Make it sparkle and shine!

Role-Play: Your aunt just gave you an ugly sweater for Christmas. With enthusiasm in your voice, practice saying thank you. It can be as simple as, "Thank you for the sweater. It is nice to know that you care about me."

Sparkle Shoes: Clean an old pair of tennis shoes with soap and water. Show those shoes how thankful you are for providing you with much adventure.

Home Organizer Hal

H HOME ORGANIZER — Hal

"I had a habit of not putting things away. My school desk was stuffed with old papers and broken pencils. My bedroom looked like a tornado went through it. One day I realized my life was not balanced. I decided to clean my bedroom and make a HOME for everything that I loved and used. I bagged 9 bags of "stuff" that I did not use and took them to a needy family. I threw away broken toys and other items that looked old. Several baskets now became the HOMES for my pencils, books, toys, and electronics. Everything that I touched would now return to its HOME. Slowing down and focusing on each moment helped me shine and feel in charge of my day."

POSITIVE SELF-TALK
"I return items to their home."

REFLECT & SHINE

- What items do you lose often? Do they have a home or place they belong?

- Can you make a HOME for them?

- Describe how organized your bedroom looks.

- Do you think you should make your bed in the morning? How can making your bed help you feel organized?

- What HOMES do you have in your desk, backpack or bedroom?

- Remembering that it takes 21 days to make or break a habit, how can you train your brain to put items back in their home?

~ ACTIVITIES ~

"Tidy room = Tidy mind"

Are you a hoarder? Do you keep "stuff" you no longer use or need? If yes, then listen up! The first thing you need to do is DECLUTTER (GET RID OF IT). Start with your bedroom (make sure to involve your parents).

MAKE 3 SIMPLE PILES:

» Keep   » Throw away   » Donate or sell

How many bags did you come up with?

Next, declutter your backpack and your desk at school. Remember to save only the items you love and use.

Once you have declutterred, the fun begins. Purchase boxes, baskets, hooks, labels, and begin making homes for your different items. Some labels may say: electronics, jewelry, hair bows, paper, homework, pencils, paperclips, art supplies, socks, pictures, cards, make-up, dirty laundry, and books.

Design a picture with the clutter from your drawer. Paint or use a colorful marker to write **"I return items to their HOME."** Say it daily until it becomes a habit.

Make a daily TO DO list of your morning, after school, and evening routines.
{ It might look like this: }

- Make bed as soon as I get up
- Shower & dress
- Eat breakfast
- Brush hair & teeth
- Put everything in bathroom back in their HOME

- Say daily affirmations
- Breathe and stretch
- Hug parents
- Pick up backpack and shoes from their daily HOME, and go to school to SHINE!

Inspiring Izzie

I INSPIRING Izzie

"I often felt invisible at school. I played alone at recess and felt left out of tag, foursquare, and conversations. On weekends, I was not invited to sleepovers or birthday parties. One day, my mother signed me up for swimming at the YMCA. I went to the pool every night to practice and felt full of energy, because I found something I loved. I was excited when I joined a swim team and started racing others. Finding my passion helped me make new friends. Now I notice when others on the playground feel left out, and I encourage them to shine by finding their passion!"

POSITIVE SELF-TALK
"I inspire others to find their passion."

REFLECT & SHINE

- Izzie's passion (something she loves) is swimming. What is your passion?

- How does it feel to be left out?

- Instead of feeling sad when you are left out, how can you reach out and make new friends?

- Why is it fun to have friends with your same passion? Why is it fun to have friends with different passions?

- What qualities do you like in a friend? How can you build a good friendship?

~ ACTIVITIES ~

"Find what brings you joy and go there."
- Jan Phillips

"You have to know what sparks the light in you so that you, in your own way, can illuminate the world."
- Oprah Winfrey

HOW CAN YOU FIND YOUR PASSION?
YOU CAN BE INSPIRED BY:

P = PICTURES – Make a collage of pictures, sayings, words, and things you love

A = ART – Paint, draw, mold, weave, color, visit an art show

S = SONG & DANCE – turn on music, play an instrument, go to a concert, dance like no one is watching

S = STILLNESS – Be still and listen to where your heart wants to go. Journal your thoughts

I = INVITING – Invite new friends in your life and be curious about their interests and passions

O = OUTSIDE – Discover the beautiful world of nature

N = NOTICING – Notice what books you are drawn to at the library

preJudged Jamal

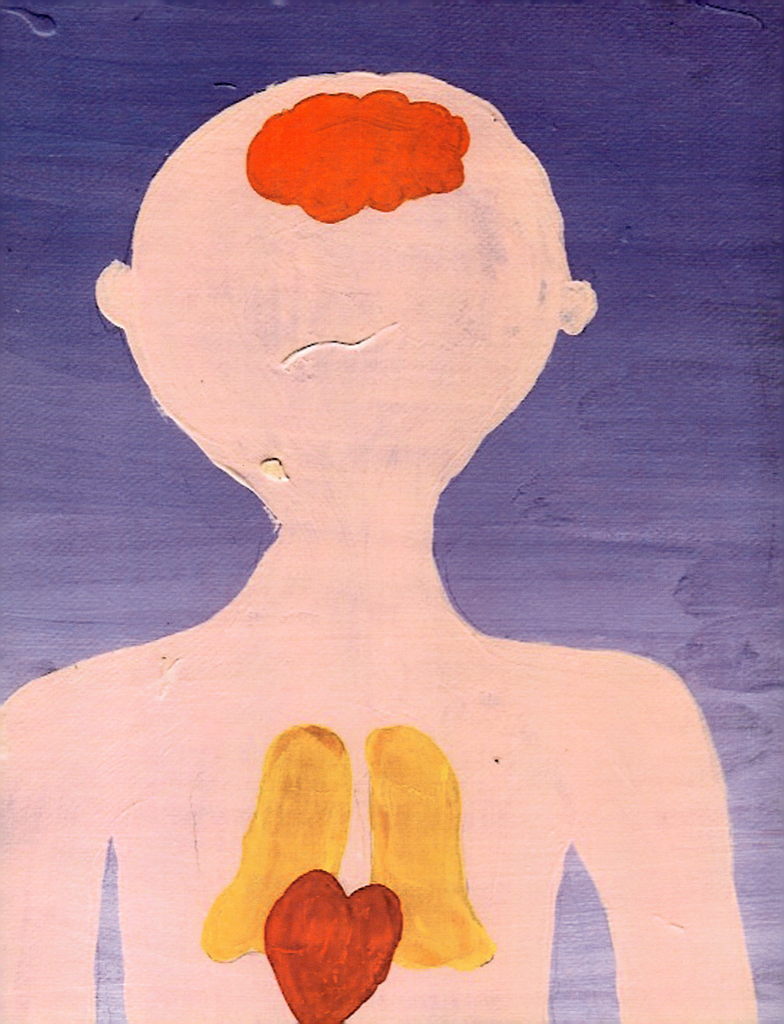

J preJUDGED Jamal

"Hi! My name is Jamal. One morning during my bus ride to school, someone refused to sit with me because of my skin color. Those words will never be forgotten. It felt like a punch in the stomach. It hurt me to think that someone was judging me before they knew me as a friend. Instead of having revenge, I recognized the kid on the bus was missing out on an awesome friend. He did not realize that we were more alike than different. Later, the boy on the bus apologized for his hurtful words. Forgiving others and believing in myself is helping me shine throughout my life."

POSITIVE SELF-TALK
"I look in the mirror before I JUDGE."

REFLECT & SHINE

- Think of how dull the world would be if we all looked, dressed, and acted the same. What differences do you see in your friends?

- We are more alike than different. How are we alike?

- Feel fortunate that you have a healthy body, brain, and home. Many children are homeless or live with disabilities causing them to look different than you. How can you volunteer or pitch in to help people with differences?

- Wayne Dyer said when you judge another, you do not define them, you define yourself. What are you saying about yourself if you call someone names?

~ ACTIVITIES ~

"Don't judge a book by its cover."
– English Proverb

Make a plaque with gold glitter using these powerful words.

THE GOLDEN RULE:
Treat Others the Way You Want to Be Treated.

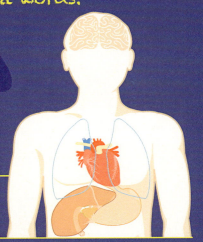

We may look different on the outside, but we have the same 7 organs.

» Label the 7 organs: brain, heart, liver, stomach, kidneys, lungs, and skin.

WEB OF CONNECTION GAME:

Form a group with the first student holding a ball of yarn in one hand and the end of the yarn in the other. Student shares one fact about themself such as, "I have blonde hair". Student gently hands ball to someone else in the group while holding end of yarn. That student shares different information about themself and then passes the ball while holding onto their piece of yarn.

A web of differences is formed. WE ARE ALL DIFFERENT, YET WE ARE CONNECTED! Now one person gently tugs on the yarn. It takes each one of us to stay connected. What happens when one person lets go of their piece of yarn?

» Use the circle to mix skin color with paint or crayons using white, brown, yellow, or pink.

DIVERSITY FAMILY TREE
Make several leaves to put on a tree branch. On each leaf write names of family members. Add pictures, words, foods, traditions, or anything that describes your family. Share your family tree proudly with your community.

Kind Karen

K Kind — Karen

"I have a hard time getting along with my older brother. He tells me I am annoying and calls me a baby. I screamed at my mom, 'It's not my fault...I don't do anything'. I can't understand why he is so mean. My parents told me if I wanted kindness from my brother, I needed to bring kindness to him. Instead of blaming him, I began to look at myself to see what I could change. I started helping my brother clean his room. I also gave him his own personal space so he would not be annoyed. Changing myself, instead of blaming him, helped my brother be more compassionate and loving toward me."

POSITIVE SELF-TALK
"I spread kindness and compassion."

REFLECT & SHINE

- Instead of blaming others, look deep inside yourself and see what you need to bring to the relationship. How can you bring kindness to those who are being mean?

- Someone who is acting mean is someone who is not happy. Why do you think some people are not happy?

- Name 5 ways to spread kindness to your community.

- Being a kind role model for younger children is important. To whom are you a role model?

~ ACTIVITIES ~

"I've learned that people will forget what you said, people will forget what you did, but people will never forget how you made them feel."
– Maya Angelou

"The Best Things in Life are Free"

» **Meet Someone New Monday:** Introduce yourself to a new friend and invite him or her to eat lunch with you. Sometimes the people who seem different than you turn out to be your best friends. Invite an unkind person to eat lunch with you. They need it the most.

» **Take Time to Forgive Tuesday:** Forgive someone who has hurt you. Ask forgiveness if you have hurt someone else. Forgive an unkind person. They need it the most.

» **Wordless Wednesday:** Show kindness with ACTIONS instead of words. Remember actions speak louder than words. Show actions to unkind people. They need it the most.

» **Thankful Thursday:** Write notes of appreciation to people who have helped you. Make them colorful and bright to bring joy. Show gratitude to unkind people. They need it the most.

» **Friendly Friday:** Give away GENUINE compliments to friends, family, and teachers. Give compliments to unkind people. They need it the most.

» **Smiling Saturday:** Smile at everyone you meet, especially if they look miserable. Smile at unkind people. They need it the most.

» **Show Love Sunday:** Give free hugs to the people who mean the most to you. The best thing you can give others is your time. Make an elderly person a cup of tea and ask them to share a favorite story. Show love to unkind people. They need it the most.

Listening Lucy

L LISTENING Lucy

"Many girls and teachers thought I was shy. Although I was known as a friend you could trust, others did not know my powerful tool was listening. My goal was to find out as much as I could about other people. I enjoyed listening and learning about others, instead of talking about myself. Being still and quiet allowed me make good decisions. I loved to go to quiet places and listen to nature. Paying attention to friends helped me shine with many caring friends."

POSITIVE SELF-TALK
"I listen to others."

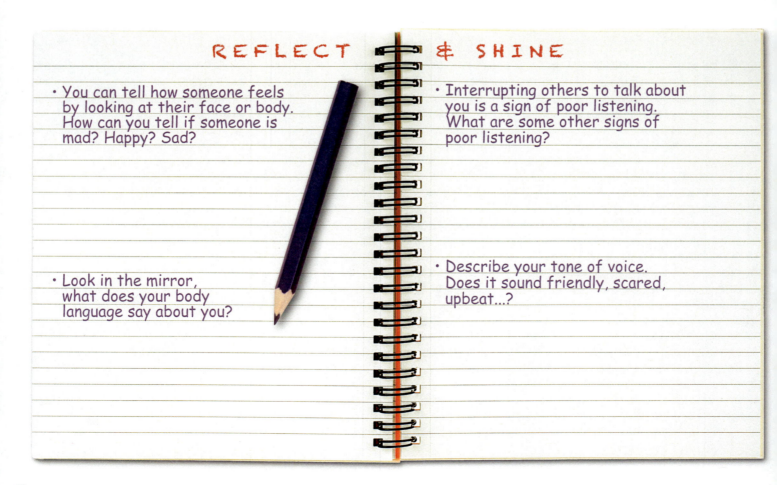

REFLECT & SHINE

- You can tell how someone feels by looking at their face or body. How can you tell if someone is mad? Happy? Sad?

- Look in the mirror, what does your body language say about you?

- Interrupting others to talk about you is a sign of poor listening. What are some other signs of poor listening?

- Describe your tone of voice. Does it sound friendly, scared, upbeat...?

~ ACTIVITIES ~

"Most people do not listen with an intent to understand. They listen with the goal to respond."
— Steven Covey

WHICH TYPE OF LISTENER ARE YOU?

FAST LISTENER: Pretending to listen, "YAH, YAH," nodding head in agreement, "OH, WOW," shoulders hunched.

REACTIVE LISTENER: DRAMA, Reacting to everything: "You are kidding me," the story becomes about you, responding without thought, interrupting to talk about yourself.

GENUINE LISTENER: Sitting up tall with shoulders back, not interrupting, making eye contact, facing person, repeating back what they say, being curious and open to seeing things in a different way.

COMMUNICATION
- Body Language 55%
- Tone 38%
- Verbal 7%

Practice Listening Without Responding:
» Buddy up with a partner and practice listening to each other for 2 minutes.
» Tell a story about a time when you got in trouble at home.
» Tell a story about a time you had a problem with a friend (no names).

5 LISTENING GUIDELINES FOR GROUPS
- Keep your eyes on the speaker
- Keep your body still
- Listening ears – you can't listen and talk at the same time
- Raise your hand if you have a question
- Never give up

BODY LANGUAGE GAME:
CAN YOU USE BODY LANGUAGE FOR THESE WORDS?

» Stop
» Look
» Be Quiet
» Listen
» That Way
» Hello
» Goodbye
» No
» Yes
» Come This Way

Mannerly Mike

M MANNERLY Mike

"My dad left me when I was little. My mom says he has some real problems, but I still want to see him. He came to see me three years ago, and we had some fun playing video games. I get excited when the phone rings thinking it might be my dad but then quickly feel disappointed when I learn it is not. I know the kids in my class get annoyed with me because I use bad language and can be pretty rude at the lunch table. One day the firefighters in our town started volunteering at my school. They played basketball with us at recess. I noticed they never used bad language and always had a smile to give me. One of the firefighters asked me to go on the fire truck with him! Every Wednesday, he taught me manners that I have used to help me form better friendships."

POSITIVE SELF-TALK
"I use manners to show respect."

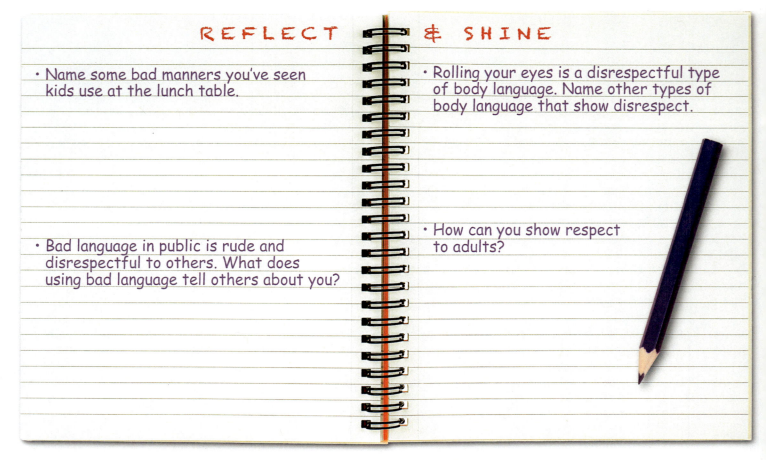

REFLECT & SHINE

- Name some bad manners you've seen kids use at the lunch table.

- Bad language in public is rude and disrespectful to others. What does using bad language tell others about you?

- Rolling your eyes is a disrespectful type of body language. Name other types of body language that show disrespect.

- How can you show respect to adults?

~ ACTIVITIES ~

"If you can't say something nice, don't say anything at all."
— Thumper from Bambi

BRING RESPECT

- **B** **Bad** Bad language is not polite. Never use it.
- **R** **Remember** Remember to say you are sorry.
- **I** **Introduce** Introduce yourself to others: Shake hands (short, firm, and solid) and make eye contact. Say: "Hello, my name is _____. What's yours?"
- **N** **Never** Never tap people on the shoulder. Be patient and wait your turn to talk.
- **G** **Give** Give thank you notes and cards to special people in your life.

- **R** **Raise** Raise your hand in class.
- **E** **Excuse Me** Use "Excuse me" when accidentally bumping into someone.
- **P** **Please** Always remember to say please and thank you.
- **E** **Everyone** Hold the door open for EVERYONE and say "After you".
- **C** **Cell** Cell phones are for safety. Put them away during family time.
- **T** **Table Manners** DO: Put both feet on floor, eat from your plate only, chew with your mouth closed, use napkin, eat slowly, sit tall, help clear table. DON'T: Burp, blow nose at table, pick your teeth, make a lot of slurping noises, chomp, leave without permission, chew with your mouth open, tell disgusting stories, wipe mouth with sleeve, put elbows on table or talk when you are chewing your food.

Noticing Naima

N NOTICING Naima

"Hi! My name is Naima. I have always been a worrier. I worried constantly about passing tests in school. I was so afraid I would fail and be left behind without my friends. Sometimes I got a huge stomach ache. When Mom would say, 'don't panic', that usually made it worse. One day my friend brought me a sparkly worry box. She told me to put all my worries in the box and place it in on a shelf. Now instead of worrying, I notice and name my feelings, then let worries stay in the box. Breathing deeply helps me to stop thinking and calm down."

POSITIVE SELF-TALK
"I notice, name, and let go of worries."

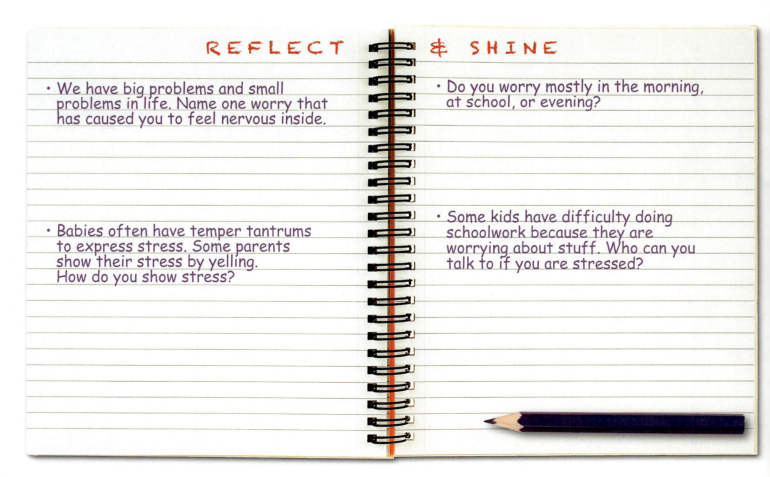

REFLECT & SHINE

- We have big problems and small problems in life. Name one worry that has caused you to feel nervous inside.

- Babies often have temper tantrums to express stress. Some parents show their stress by yelling. How do you show stress?

- Do you worry mostly in the morning, at school, or evening?

- Some kids have difficulty doing schoolwork because they are worrying about stuff. Who can you talk to if you are stressed?

~ ACTIVITIES ~

*"Feelings are just visitors.
Let them come and go."*
— Mooji

WORRY BOX: Decorate the outside of a small box with glitter, beads, shells, or any item that sparks your interest. Place written worries in box and put a lid on it! Place box on a high shelf and let go of them.

STEPS TO CALM A BIG WORRY

1. Sit up tall and breathe in through your nose for 4 seconds. Hold your breath for 2 seconds. Exhale slowly through your nose for 4 seconds. Repeat 5-10 times.
2. Write worst thing that could happen and best thing that could happen. Which one is more likely?
3. Before falling asleep, think of all the things you are grateful for and say them out loud.

SAFE PLACE

Close your eyes and think of a time you felt happy. Picture that place in your mind. What sounds do you hear? What smells? What can you touch? What is happening around you? Who are you with? Go to that safe place now in your thoughts.

"CATCH YOUR WORRIES"

Make your own personalized dream catcher to catch your worries, fears, negative thoughts, and nightmares.

MATERIALS REQUIRED:
Yarn
Margarine lid (or store bought round hoop)
Beads
Scissors
Feathers
String

Cut out the inside of a margarine lid, leaving a circular ring. Use yarn to cover the round ring. Use any string and create a web in the middle of the ring. Decorate with feathers, beads, family names. Hang above your bed to catch your worries!

Optimistic
Oreto

O OPTIMISTIC Oreta

"Everyone wonders why I show up everyday living life FULL ON. It's not because I have dealt with a condition known as Cystic Fibrosis since birth, or because I end up in the hospital fighting for my life. It is not because I listen to my mom cry at night for fear something bad is happening to me. It is 100% because I make a choice every morning to choose happiness. I change my negative thoughts (pessimistic) to positive thoughts (optimistic). I hope for a miracle and choose to make each and every moment my best. I don't blame others or feel sorry for myself. I love to try anything that people tell me is impossible like headstands or scorpion pose. Yoga has been my inspiration. I know that anything is possible and miracles do happen. Changing negative thoughts to positive thoughts allows me to shine daily!"

POSITIVE SELF-TALK
"I live life full ON."

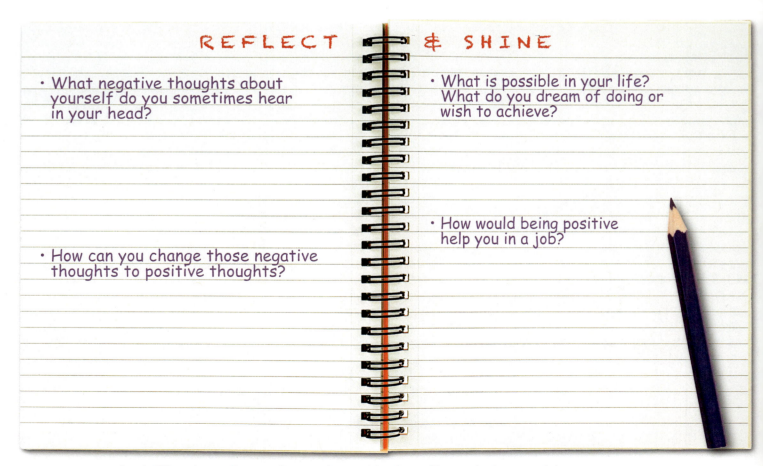

REFLECT & SHINE

- What negative thoughts about yourself do you sometimes hear in your head?

- How can you change those negative thoughts to positive thoughts?

- What is possible in your life? What do you dream of doing or wish to achieve?

- How would being positive help you in a job?

Cystic Fibrosis - a disease, few are born with, that affects the lungs and digestive system.

~ ACTIVITIES ~

*"Watch your thoughts – for they become your words.
Watch your words – for they become your actions.
Watch your actions – for they become your character.
Watch your character – it becomes your destiny."*
— Lao Tzu

HALF EMPTY / HALF FULL: Place a glass in front of you and fill it halfway with water. Is the glass half empty or half full? Do you say, "Oh, it's just terrible that I have a half empty glass (negative)". Or do you say, "Oh, it is wonderful that I have a half full glass (optimistic)".

You can't change other people, but you can control yourself and your thoughts.

Which of these thoughts are OPTIMISTIC?

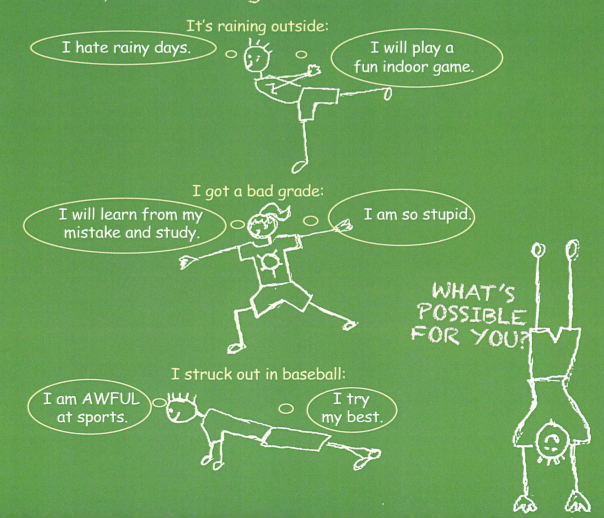

It's raining outside:
- I hate rainy days.
- I will play a fun indoor game.

I got a bad grade:
- I will learn from my mistake and study.
- I am so stupid.

I struck out in baseball:
- I am AWFUL at sports.
- I try my best.

WHAT'S POSSIBLE FOR YOU?

Pausing Pablo

P PAUSING Pablo

"Have you ever been so angry that you feel like your head is going to pop off? My name is Pablo, and some of my friends tell me I have anger issues. One day I was lining up for recess and my good friend, Tommy, cut me in line. I got so angry that I gave him a strong push. Tommy fell down, hurt his head, and had to go to the nurse's office. I felt like the worst person ever! I yelled out, 'I wasn't thinking!' That was when I knew I needed to train my brain to PAUSE before I hurt someone else.
Now when I feel my body getting angry, I PAUSE - RELAX MY BODY - AND BREATHE. I know anger will come and go but instead of reacting, I will shine by pausing."

POSITIVE SELF-TALK
"I pause, relax, and breathe."

REFLECT & SHINE

- Being impulsive is when you do the first thing that pops into your head instead of pausing. Tell about a time you were impulsive.

- Explain how your face, hands, heart, mouth and body react to anger.

- Tense your body. Feel it get tight. Now relax your body and breathe deep. Feel the power within to calm yourself. What will you do next time you feel anger?

- Anger is ENERGY. Instead of hurting others or yourself when you are angry, what can you do with anger that is safe?

~ ACTIVITIES ~

"Life is 10% what happened to you and 90% how you react."
- Lou Holtz

WHICH SIGNALS BELOW HAPPEN IN YOUR BODY WHEN YOU ARE ANGRY?

- Tight body
- Pumping heart
- THROW something
- Sweaty palms
- Dizzy head
- Can't think
- CRUSHING hands
- EXPLODING BODY
- Red face
- Bad thoughts
- Untrue words
- Throw up
- Want to hurt yourself
- BREAK SOMETHING
- Something evil is controlling you
- ATTACK
- Tense body
- Knotted stomach
- ENERGY
- STRONG body
- Knees buckle
- REVENGE
- Faint
- Lose voice
- Headache
- Stomach ache
- HOT
- Cry
- Legs get numb
- Hold breath
- Feel like a bad person

THE 3 ANGER RULES:
Don't hurt others. Don't hurt yourself. Don't break things.

YOU CAN TALK IT OUT, THINK IT OUT, OR PLAY IT OUT.

Choose if the following actions go under "talking", "thinking", or "playing".

- Go to a quiet place and read
- Run
- Draw
- Bike
- Swim
- Jump on trampoline
- Go outside
- Ignore
- Watch TV
- Rest
- Listen to music
- Play with pets
- Play drums
- Punch a ball
- Sing
- Dance
- Build something
- Clean something
- Shop
- Ride scooter
- Talk to friend
- Climb a tree
- Be alone
- Walk
- Talk to your family about your feelings
- Breathe & stretch
- Punch a pillow
- Play with sibling
- Play a game
- Think
- Meditate
- Pray
- Play football
- LET IT GO
- Imagine you are in a different place
- Squeeze hands into a fist
- Think about a favorite thing
- Take a cold shower
- Write an angry letter and throw it away
- Squeeze toes together
- Go on the computer & play game
- Cry – let it out
- Walk and talk

Quieting Quin

Q QUIETING — Quin

"I often hear my parents fighting late at night. I hate the sound of the harsh words, and it feels icky inside my body. At first, I tried to stop them, but that usually made it worse, and they would just yell, 'Go to your room, Quin.' The fighting in my house would often travel in my brain when I went to school. It made me feel angry inside until I discovered the power of quieting myself. I found a pair of headphones so I could play music when the fights started. I surrounded myself with things I loved like books, stuffed animals, and my journal. Instead of listening to adult problems, I zone into what I love and focus on my breathing. Now I don't carry the fighting in my head, and I can shine because I know how to quiet my brain."

POSITIVE SELF-TALK
"I quiet myself."

REFLECT & SHINE

- Many families have disagreements. How can you block out the sounds you don't want to hear?

- Think of a time you were quiet in your bedroom doing something that you loved. What were you doing?

- Where do you feel most peaceful?

- Who can you talk to if you are upset?

~ ACTIVITIES ~

"In the midst of movement and chaos, keep stillness inside you."
— Deepok Chopra

QUIET SEATED POSE:

Cross your legs, press your sit bones down and lift the crown of your head to sky. Interlace fingers behind you and breathe here for 5-10 breaths. Then, inhale and fold over your crossed legs. Close your eyes and breathe here 5-10 breaths. Quiet yourself and listen to your breath.

Calming Jar:

MATERIALS REQUIRED
- Small Plastic Bottle
- ½ Bottle Filled With Karo Syrup or Honey
- ½ Bottle of Warm Water
- 1 Tablespoon of Neon Ultra Fine Glitter
- 2 Heaping Tablespoons of Clear Gel Glue
- Super Glue (for lids)

DIRECTIONS

Mix all ingredients and put lid on bottle. Super glue lid shut and let dry.

Shake up and let the calming begin.

» **Star Gaze/Cloud Gaze:** Star gaze and marvel at the vastness of the billions of stars above you. Lay in the grass and watch the clouds quietly pass. Do you recognize any pictures or shapes?

» **Relaxation Stones:** Collect smooth stones. Paint peaceful words or pictures with acrylic paint. Spray stones with clear gloss to protect.

» **Calming Spray:** Mix distilled water with a tablespoon rubbing alcohol in small glass spray bottle. Add 20-30 drops of lavender oil. Spray in air, away from eyes.

R REPORTING   Roxy

"I hate it when others don't follow the rules. I think they should be punished. It took some time for me to realize that telling on others never really solved the problem. It usually just made everyone mad. Instead of being known as a tattletale, I wanted to be known as a reporter. I began finding the good stuff in everyone and excitedly told my teacher and others what I found. It was easy to notice others who were kind and nice. Reporting good behavior changed the feeling in my class, and the kids started getting along. Recess became fun, and I started playing with new friends. But always remember the two most important reporting rules: ALWAYS report DANGER AND BULLIES to adults. When I found the magical tool of reporting the good in others, I began to shine in my class and with my friends."

POSITIVE SELF-TALK
" I report the goodness in others."

REFLECT & SHINE

- Reporting good behavior allows you and others to shine. What good behaviors do you see in others?

- Always report danger. Name 5 dangerous behaviors you would report to an adult.

- Always report bullies. When have you witnessed bullying?

- Name 5 different people you could report danger to in your community.

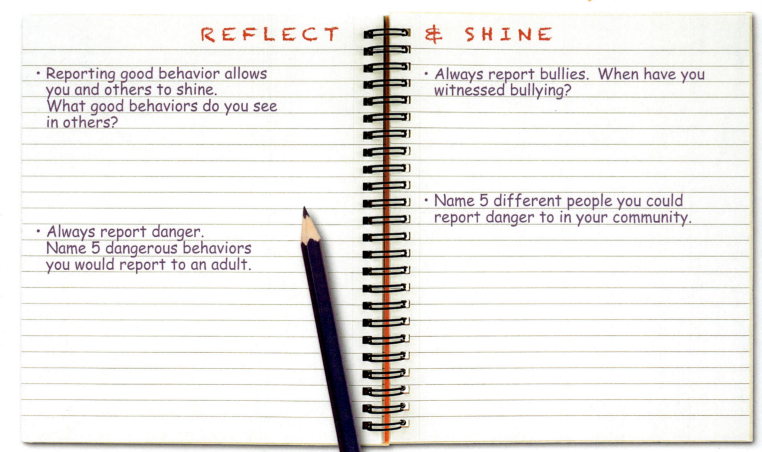

~ ACTIVITIES ~

"Strong people don't put others down, they lift them up."
– Michael P. Watson

REPORTING GUIDELINES

>> 1 Solve problems independently first. If problems continue, seek help from a trusted adult.
>> 2 Report danger.
>> 3 Report someone who <u>continually</u> makes you feel scared, embarrassed, left out, or sad.
>> 4 Report students who make GOOD choices.

Report / Tattle Quiz:
(Remember to report danger, bullies, and good things.)

Put the letter R in front of Reports and a T in front of Tattles.

_____ Roxy cut in front of me in line.

_____ A man tried to give me candy near his car when I was walking home.

_____ Roxy listened to the substitute teacher while you were gone.

_____ Roxy is walking across the top of the monkey bars.

_____ Roxy said a bad word.

_____ Roxy is being mean to me for the first time.

_____ Roxy is mean to me every day. I told her to stop, and she keeps kicking me when no one is looking. I am scared of her.

_____ Roxy didn't finish her work.

_____ Roxy embarrasses me in front of everyone and makes me feel left out. She tells others not be my friend. I see her laughing and pointing at me. I am alone.

_____ Roxy told me she was going to get me after school and to watch out!

_____ Roxy helped me at recess when I fell down.

Stand Up Stella

S STAND UP Stella

"When I was in kindergarten, a new student who spoke only a little English started school in the middle of the year. Another classmate, Billy, started calling him names every day. He did it during recess, and when the teacher wasn't looking. I could tell by the look on the new student's face that he was scared of Billy. I went right up to Billy and looked him straight in the eye and told him he needed to stop, or I would report him to the teacher. I know the new student was thankful for my help. I felt good inside knowing that I could stand tall and shine by helping a classmate."

POSITIVE SELF-TALK
"I stand up for others and myself."

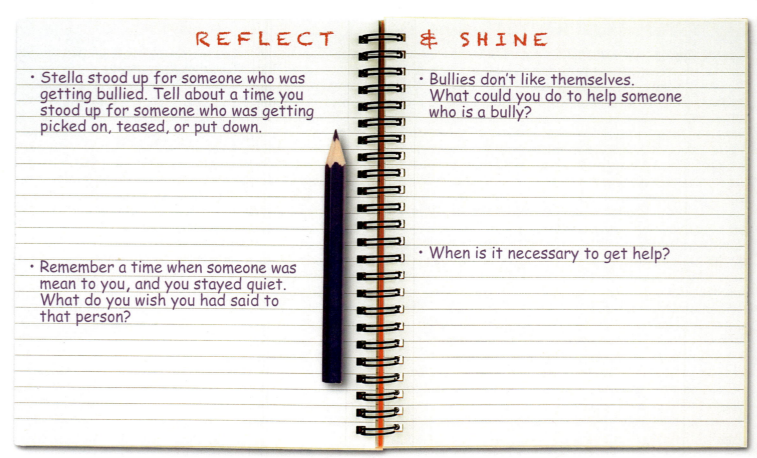

REFLECT & SHINE

- Stella stood up for someone who was getting bullied. Tell about a time you stood up for someone who was getting picked on, teased, or put down.

- Remember a time when someone was mean to you, and you stayed quiet. What do you wish you had said to that person?

- Bullies don't like themselves. What could you do to help someone who is a bully?

- When is it necessary to get help?

~ ACTIVITIES ~

"No one has the power to ruin your day."
- Lizzie Sider

WHY DO KIDS BULLY?

Someone else has bullied him/her.
To get revenge on someone who has hurt him/her.
They don't like themselves.
They feel they will be liked if they put others down.
They want attention and power.

IF YOU ARE BULLIED, YOU CAN:

Tell the bully to STOP.
Be DIRECT with your words.
Ignore and go the other way.
Stay with your friends or group.
Distract bully by laughing or making a joke.
Apologize if you have done something to cause hurt.
Stand tall and believe in yourself.
Understand why people bully.
Talk to your parents.
REPORT

Words by Unknown:

I will not take these words inside.
I will not let them hurt my pride.
I know I'm not a perfect kid,
But your words don't fit what I did.
I will not take these words inside.
I will not let them hurt my pride.

Tenacious Tim

T TENACIOUS Tim

"Most friends freak out when they have a problem or something doesn't go their way. I think I'm the weirdo who embraces challenges. Math is my favorite subject because all problems can be solved. It is the same with LIFE. Challenges may be hard and may take time to figure out, but if I stick with solving them, I'll be fine. I don't wait for others to solve my challenges in school. I think of solutions and solve them peacefully myself. Problems often happen because I want the same thing as someone else. When this happens, I know I can share, trade, take turns, talk it out, move away, or get help! I don't sit back and fear problems; I face them head on! I always find something good, even in the worst situations!"

 **POSITIVE SELF-TALK**
"I try different solutions."

REFLECT & SHINE

- Many kids fear problems and give up when things don't work out the first time. Name a movie or book character who never gave up.

- Challenge creates change. What subject in school is difficult for you and requires you to be tenacious?

- Having a "stick with it" attitude is important when we are faced with problems in life. When have you wanted to give up?

- What playground or home problem have you solved on your own?

~ ACTIVITIES ~

*"Most people spend more time
and energy going around problems
than in trying to solve them.*

- Henry Ford

PROBLEM SOLVING WITH ONE PERSON:

KEEP, START, STOP
(quick powerful words
to express your needs)

KEEP: What do you want the other person to KEEP doing? _____
_____

START: What do you want the other person to START doing? _____
_____

STOP: What do you want the other person to STOP doing? _____
_____

POWERFUL I STATEMENTS:
(INSTEAD OF YOU -
BLAMING STATEMENTS)

I feel (name the feeling) _____
_____

When you (describe the action) _____
_____

Will you please (tell what you want the other person to do) _____
_____

PROBLEM SOLVING WITH A GROUP:
(solving a problem TOGETHER is more powerful than solving a problem ALONE):

STEPS	EXAMPLE
1. State Problem	There are too many bad words in our school
2. Brainstorm Ideas	Punish kids, make them apologize, call parents, all kids sign pledge to not swear
3. Judge Ideas	Evaluate all ideas
4. Choose Best Solution	Group decides to create a school pledge
5. Take Action	Share pledge with school

Unmovable Uriel

U UNMOVABLE — Uriel

"Many of my friends were choosing to stay up all night playing online video games instead of doing homework or studying for tests. I noticed these tired friends goofing off in class and cheating in order to pass tests. My dream was to play sports in high school, so I was determined to keep a clean school record. Many friends would pressure me to join in, but I kept my head high and concentrated on keeping my good grades, staying out of trouble, and playing my guitar. Being UNMOVED by negative peer pressure helped me shine in school and in sports!"

POSITIVE SELF-TALK
"I am unmoved by negative peer pressure."

REFLECT & SHINE

- Most kids want to be liked by other kids their own age. They want to "fit in". What do you notice kids doing to fit in?

- Why do you suppose people making poor decisions want you to join in with them?

- Sometimes a group does not always make good decisions. When have you followed the group and discovered their decisions were not right?

- Do you consider yourself a follower or leader?

~ ACTIVITIES ~

"When your friends are looking for trouble, go the other way."
— Unknown

PEER PRESSURE: When you feel someone in your age group pushing you towards a certain choice. (Positive or Negative)

PUT A CHECK IN FRONT OF PEER PRESSURE THAT IS POSITIVE.

_____ Your friends are pressuring you to run a 5K race.
_____ Your friends are excluding someone who acts different.
_____ Your friends are cheating.
_____ Your friends are raising money for a needy family.
_____ Your friends are starting a book club.
_____ Your friends are pressuring you to goof off in class.
_____ Your friends are cheering for struggling kids.

PEER PRESSURE TIPS
Stand tall and look people in the eye.
Tell others how you feel.
Remember your power within and believe in yourself.
Walk away or just say no to negative pressure.
Find friends who push you to positive choices.

PEER PRESSURE PRACTICE: HOW DO YOU HANDLE THE FOLLOWING SITUATIONS?

1. You are failing reading and your friend has a cheat sheet to use on the next test. She says everyone does it and it is fine. How do you respond?

2. There is a substitute teacher in your room. Many are being silly and not following the rules. They are giving you the "look" to join in. What do you do?

Valuing Van

VALUING — Van

"I live in a small house with seven siblings. My dad fixes old beat up cars, and my mom takes care of us. Even though my parents do not have money to go on cool vacations, I travel around the world through books. Every night my mom yells, 'Van, quit reading those books and go to bed!' Books take me to deserts, tall mountains, blue oceans, and dark forests. The public library lets me borrow books every week for free! I love that! I love learning as much as I can from my teachers and others around me. I dream of getting a good job in my future and visiting the places I read about. I am saving for college by cutting my neighbor's grass. Valuing education helps me shine and think about all the opportunities and possibilities that are ahead in my life."

 **POSITIVE SELF-TALK** "I value education."

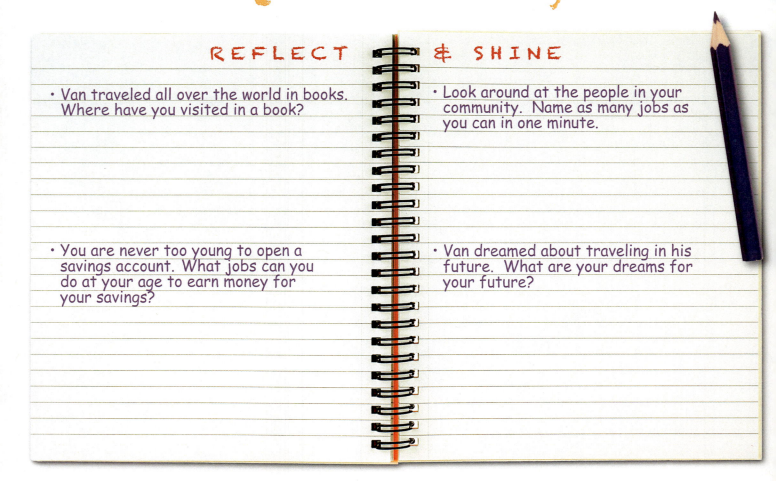

REFLECT & SHINE

- Van traveled all over the world in books. Where have you visited in a book?

- Look around at the people in your community. Name as many jobs as you can in one minute.

- You are never too young to open a savings account. What jobs can you do at your age to earn money for your savings?

- Van dreamed about traveling in his future. What are your dreams for your future?

~ ACTIVITIES ~

"Either you run the day, or the day runs you."
— Jim Rohn

FUTURE CHECK: Do you know what kind of job you want in your future? Place a check next to what is most important to you.

- _____ Computers
- _____ Taking care of sick people
- _____ Selling things
- _____ Building things
- _____ Fixing things
- _____ Problem solving
- _____ Teaching others
- _____ Being outside
- _____ Working with money
- _____ Drawing, Painting, Music, Sports
- _____ Working with animals

GOAL SETTING FOR THE NEW YEAR

Choose one word for what you want MORE and one word for what you want LESS in your life? Remember you can't change others – ONLY YOURSELF. Goal set with your family, classmates, and friends.

NAME_____

GOALS FOR THE YEAR 20____

MORE_____

LESS_____

WORD BANK: love, respect, honesty, responsibility, reading, time with family, studying, goofing off, music, listening, focusing, gossip, mean words, sports, video games, texting, excluding others, swear words, art, worrying, quiet times, giving, helping, dancing, laughing

HOLIDAY GOAL SETTING TRADITION

On New Year's Eve, write a letter to yourself. Remember special events, accomplishments, new friendships, or travel. Include a bucket list for the following year of goals you set for yourself. Place this letter in your "holiday decorations" box so you will find it the following year.

Wondrous Will

W WONDROUS — Will

"I was in kindergarten when my mom died. I know most parents don't die at a young age, but mine was sick and could not get better. I cried for days and let myself feel sad. It helped me to go back to school and focus on my work. My friends looked out for me when I got sad. One friend always said to me, "I am here for you." I don't like to talk about it much, but I do understand that little kids are curious and want to know what happened. It helps me to have pictures of my mom in my room to imagine that she is always with me. I love to go to the cemetery and talk to her, especially on her birthday. I notice at the cemetery that I am not the only person who has lost someone they loved. I usually bring a cake and celebrate her awesomeness. Now that I am older, I know each day is a wondrous journey."

POSITIVE SELF-TALK
"I love this wondrous life."

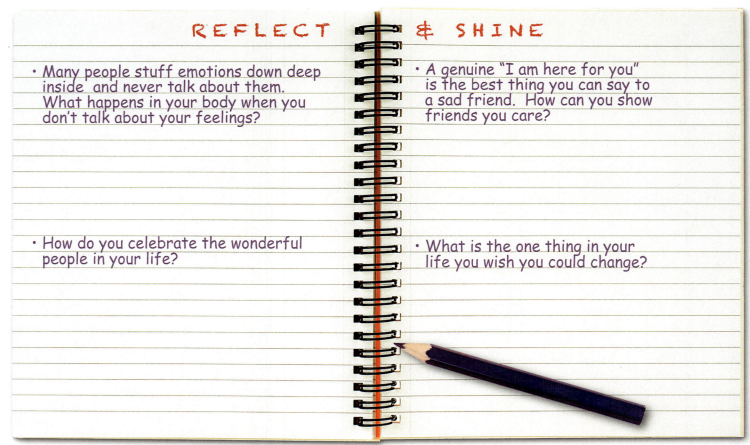

REFLECT & SHINE

- Many people stuff emotions down deep inside and never talk about them. What happens in your body when you don't talk about your feelings?

- A genuine "I am here for you" is the best thing you can say to a sad friend. How can you show friends you care?

- How do you celebrate the wonderful people in your life?

- What is the one thing in your life you wish you could change?

~ ACTIVITIES ~

"The best and most beautiful things in life cannot be seen, not touched, but are felt in the heart."
– Helen Keller

STEPS TO COPE WITH LOSS:

- Move slowly and notice the feelings surrounded by loss. Don't hide your feelings.
- Make a memory box or shelf with pictures and favorite memory items.
- Talk about the person or animal and celebrate their awesomeness.
- Surround yourself with family and friends.
- Choose to live your life to the fullest.
- Stay motivated. Set goals for yourself and reach them.

JOURNALING. Journaling is a powerful tool used to notice, name and let go of feelings. Use colorful markers to name your feelings such as blue for sad, red for anger, green for jealous, yellow for happy, and orange for worry. Notice how your feelings change. Journal your favorite memories.

WALK AND TALK. Buy a pair of walking shoes and get moving. Walking and talking is a powerful habit that all families can share together. Enjoy talking about feelings and daily events.

CREATE A MEMORY ROCK GARDEN

Purchase small, smooth rocks and use puffy paint to write the name of your loved one. Place rock under a quiet tree and visit often.

HEALING HERB GARDEN

Plant herbs in pots or a small garden. Dig in the dirt with your hands and connect with the earth. Find joy in the aroma of mint, lemongrass, thyme, or other herbs.

Xtra Effort
Xaiden

X XTRA EFFORT — Xaiden

"I was told at a young age that I had a learning problem. Just hearing those words made me feel like I was dumb and had no chance of getting smart. I put forth little effort in school because I didn't think it would matter. I went through most of my grades thinking I would always be the slow one in class. One day, I needed to do well on a math test, or I would fail. I decided to study and give it all my effort. I studied for hours with a tutor. For practice, I pretended I was teaching the difficult math lesson to others who were struggling. This helped me understand what I was learning. When I received my test back, the teacher told me I got the highest grade in the class. I am pretty sure I screamed out loud. It was then I discovered the power of effort. If I brought effort and energy to school, I could shine. Now I know that I am not dumb, and that I just learn and study differently than other kids."

 **POSITIVE SELF-TALK** "I bring extra effort."

REFLECT & SHINE

- Everyone learns differently. Do you learn best by seeing, hearing, or doing?
- How do you memorize facts?

- Everyone in life has difficult times. What is difficult for you?
- Laziness gives no reward. How do you reward yourself when you have worked hard?

~ ACTIVITIES ~

"The only place success comes before work is in the dictionary"
– Vince Lombardi

MEMORIZATION TIPS: Circle 5 that are NOT good study tips.

- Study and put most difficult facts under your pillow at night.
- Put facts in Ziploc bag and study them in your pool, hot tub, or shower.
- Wait until the morning of the test to study.
- Use a highlighter to color important words.
- Write facts down until you fill the page. Say them out loud.
- Make sure your room is clean before studying.
- Skip breakfast in order to study.
- Write facts on bathroom mirror with washable marker.
- Study with friends who goof off.
- Go on YouTube and find different teachers or music.
- Pretend like you are teaching someone.
- Stay up late watching TV before the day of the test.
- Make an acronym with words like ROYGBIV (red, orange, yellow, green, blue, indigo, violet – colors of the rainbow).
- Study on your bed surrounded by toys. Make sure lamp is far from you.
- Take short breaks. Reward yourself when you are successful.

HOW ARE YOUR STUDY HABITS? Rate yourself as Excellent, So-So, or Poor

_____ I come to school every day on time.
_____ I listen carefully when my teacher is talking.
_____ I complete my classwork and homework.
_____ I have respect for my teacher, friends, and myself.
_____ I set goals for myself.
_____ I study before tests.
_____ I balance my time. I work hard first and then play.
_____ I avoid distractions when studying.
_____ I give 100% effort and never give up!
_____ I ask others for help when needed.

Yessing Yula

Y YESSING Yula

"I was the kid who chose to miss out on birthday parties because of fear. I was afraid that others might treat me meanly or not include me. One weekend, a friend invited me to an ice skating party. I did not want to miss out on this new adventure, so I decided to face my fears and said YES! My heart was racing, and I felt fear racing through my veins as my mom dropped me off at the ice skating rink. At first, I fell many times on the ice. By the end of the night, I was skating without help and feeling excited. I met new friends while trying something new. Next time when someone asks me to try a new adventure, I will say YES and shine while facing my fears!"

POSITIVE SELF-TALK
"I say Yes to Adventure."

REFLECT & SHINE

- Tell about a time you felt scared when trying something new.

- Saying yes to making new friends can be scary. How can you invite new friends into your life?

- When is it good to say NO to something new?

- What would you do if you weren't afraid?

- Face your fears and try something you are scared to do. What courageous, new adventure would you like to try in life?

~ ACTIVITIES ~

"You can never cross the ocean until you have the courage to lose sight of the shore."
- Christopher Columbus

SAYING YES DANCE GAME: Make a standing circle. Turn on fun music. One person will go in the middle of the circle and demonstrate a dance move. All other members will copy the dance move. The person in the middle then chooses someone else to go in the middle and demonstrate a different dance move. Have fun trying something new. Just say YES! Continue until everyone has had a chance to be the dance leader.

"Courage and Fear" - Michael H. Popkin
Courage first met fear when I was still a child;
Courage gazed with cool, clear eyes; fear was something wild.
Courage urged, "Let's go ahead;" fear said, "Let's turn back."
Courage spoke of what we had, fear of what we lacked.
Courage took me by the hand and warmed my frozen bones;
Yet fear the while tugged at my legs and whispered, "We're alone."
Many have been the obstacles since first I had to choose;
And sometimes when courage led me on, I've come up with a bruise.
And many have been challenges since fear and courage met;
And yet those times I've followed Fear, too often – tagged along regret.

My Bucket List: Make a list of new things you would like to try this year: Check them off as you do them and feel courageous for trying something new. Here are some ideas: fly a kite, run in a race, sing in the shower, play an instrument, dance in the aisle at the grocery store, try a new cookie recipe, go ice skating.

Do you have the courage to stay in plank pose for one minute?

Say yes to a handstand.

Zoned In

Zeb

Z ZONED IN Zeb

"I am the kid in class who always gets in trouble. If you walked by my room you would hear 'Zeb, get quiet!' Or 'Zeb, get your work done!' I have trouble staying focused when things get hard or boring. I hear every flickering sound in my room, and my mind wonders what I can do when I get home. To help me learn focus and self-control, I practice breathing and stretching. Deep breathing while focusing on one object allows my body to be still and brings much needed oxygen to parts of my brain. Practicing this exercise daily increases my concentration and trains my brain to GET IN THE ZONE. When I feel the need to move in class, I wiggle my toes in my shoes or twiddle my thumbs under my desk. Now when I feel myself get off track, I tell my body to get in the zone and get it done!"

POSITIVE SELF-TALK
"I get in the zone."

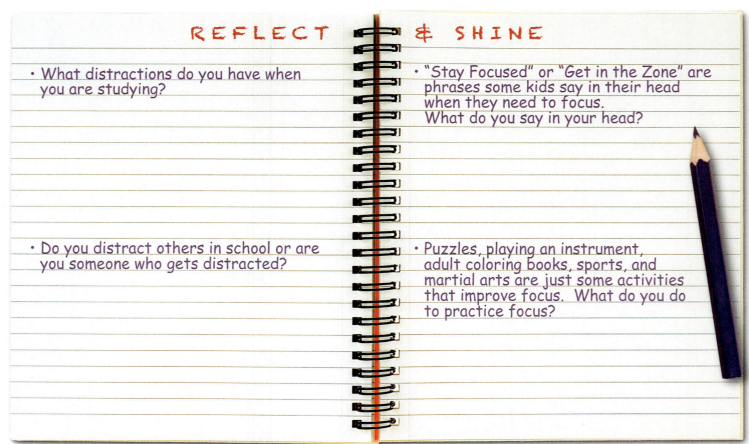

REFLECT & SHINE

- What distractions do you have when you are studying?

- Do you distract others in school or are you someone who gets distracted?

- "Stay Focused" or "Get in the Zone" are phrases some kids say in their head when they need to focus. What do you say in your head?

- Puzzles, playing an instrument, adult coloring books, sports, and martial arts are just some activities that improve focus. What do you do to practice focus?

~ ACTIVITIES ~

"The successful warrior is the average man, with laser-like focus."
- Bruce Lee

GET IN THE ZONE:
Focus on the now.
Breathe through nose filling up lungs fully with oxygen and exhale through nose slowly.
Keep your eyes on one object and ignore distractions.
Smile & never give up!

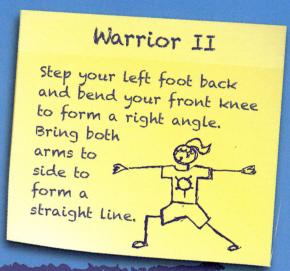

Warrior II
Step your left foot back and bend your front knee to form a right angle. Bring both arms to side to form a straight line.

PRACTICE LASER-LIKE FOCUS:

- Place a flower (or any object) at the front of the room.
- Position yourself in Warrior II pose with front fingers pointed to flower.
- Set timer for 1-2 minutes.
- Stay focused on flower. If you notice your mind getting distracted, bring your attention back to the flower.
- When timer goes off, stand tall and close your eyes. Keep your thoughts on the flower. Switch sides.
- The purpose of this activity is to notice when your mind wanders off and bring your attention back to the flower. This is where focus is strengthened. Practice daily.

VARIATIONS:

- Use same laser-like focus in tree pose. Take your gaze slowly to the ceiling and try closing your eyes.
- Try other balancing poses such as eagle, dancer, or single knee bend. Go to powerfulyou.info to learn more.

Take this same laser-like focus to your schoolwork, sport, or any activity.

ACKNOWLEDGEMENTS

"In life you will realize there is a role for everyone you meet. Some will test you, some will use you, some will love you, and some will teach you. But the ones who are truly important are the ones who bring out the best in you."
- unknown

- Rebecca Wells from Wells Marketing for gently holding my hand and guiding me through the book publishing experience with total commitment, knowledge, and genuine care. Thank you for believing in me!

- David B. Lee Creative Design for cleverly designing Powerful You.

- Green Monkey Yoga for giving me the gift of yoga. I am forever thankful for every instructor and student I breathe next to on the mat.

- Arliss Dahl Perriello for lovingly taking me under her wing and teaching me the magical art of being an elementary school counselor.

- Collier County Counselors for cheering me on.

- Cheryl Wellman from Cherelle Art for inspiring me to paint!

- Students and staff from Naples Park Elementary for showing up and shining!

- Diane Durante from Anchor Counseling for freely sharing.

- The following artists for their drawings: Allison Stevens, Noe Avila, Sofia Calle, Kaltrina Lici, Kayla Briones, Seama Tyrell, Derrick Joseph, Gabriel Velez, Yuliana Azpeitia Cruz, Mia Caputo, Jake Haven, Jyanesa Tersy, Mariah Williams, Zoe Ciabaton, Madisyn Piglia, Abby Ciabaton, Ally Steber, Kendra Kleinknecht, and Antonio Licout.

- All my friends & family who have stuck with me on this journey. Thank you, Mom!